House Hearing, 110th Congress: Vulture Funds and the Threat to Debt Relief in Africa: A Call to Action at the G-8 and Beyond

U.S. Government Printing Office (GPO)

The BiblioGov Project is an effort to expand awareness of the public documents and records of the U.S. Government via print publications. In broadening the public understanding of government and its work, an enlightened democracy can grow and prosper. Ranging from historic Congressional Bills to the most recent Budget of the United States Government, the BiblioGov Project spans a wealth of government information. These works are now made available through an environmentally friendly, print-on-demand basis, using only what is necessary to meet the required demands of an interested public. We invite you to learn of the records of the U.S. Government, heightening the knowledge and debate that can lead from such publications.

Included are the following Collections:

Budget of The United States Government
Presidential Documents
United States Code
Education Reports from ERIC
GAO Reports
History of Bills
House Rules and Manual
Public and Private Laws

Code of Federal Regulations
Congressional Documents
Economic Indicators
Federal Register
Government Manuals
House Journal
Privacy act Issuances
Statutes at Large

VULTURE FUNDS AND THE THREAT TO DEBT RELIEF IN AFRICA: A CALL TO ACTION AT THE G-8 AND BEYOND

HEARING

BEFORE THE

SUBCOMMITTEE ON AFRICA AND GLOBAL HEALTH

OF THE

COMMITTEE ON FOREIGN AFFAIRS
HOUSE OF REPRESENTATIVES

ONE HUNDRED TENTH CONGRESS

FIRST SESSION

MAY 22, 2007

Serial No. 110–72

Printed for the use of the Committee on Foreign Affairs

Available via the World Wide Web: http://www.foreignaffairs.house.gov/

U.S. GOVERNMENT PRINTING OFFICE

35–672PDF   WASHINGTON : 2007

For sale by the Superintendent of Documents, U.S. Government Printing Office
Internet: bookstore.gpo.gov   Phone: toll free (866) 512–1800; DC area (202) 512–1800
Fax: (202) 512–2250   Mail: Stop SSOP, Washington, DC 20402–0001

COMMITTEE ON FOREIGN AFFAIRS

TOM LANTOS, California, *Chairman*

HOWARD L. BERMAN, California
GARY L. ACKERMAN, New York
ENI F.H. FALEOMAVAEGA, American Samoa
DONALD M. PAYNE, New Jersey
BRAD SHERMAN, California
ROBERT WEXLER, Florida
ELIOT L. ENGEL, New York
BILL DELAHUNT, Massachusetts
GREGORY W. MEEKS, New York
DIANE E. WATSON, California
ADAM SMITH, Washington
RUSS CARNAHAN, Missouri
JOHN S. TANNER, Tennessee
GENE GREEN, Texas
LYNN C. WOOLSEY, California
SHEILA JACKSON LEE, Texas
RUBEN HINOJOSA, Texas
JOSEPH CROWLEY, New York
DAVID WU, Oregon
BRAD MILLER, North Carolina
LINDA T. SANCHEZ, California
DAVID SCOTT, Georgia
JIM COSTA, California
ALBIO SIRES, New Jersey
GABRIELLE GIFFORDS, Arizona
RON KLEIN, Florida

ILEANA ROS-LEHTINEN, Florida
CHRISTOPHER H. SMITH, New Jersey
DAN BURTON, Indiana
ELTON GALLEGLY, California
DANA ROHRABACHER, California
DONALD A. MANZULLO, Illinois
EDWARD R. ROYCE, California
STEVE CHABOT, Ohio
THOMAS G. TANCREDO, Colorado
RON PAUL, Texas
JEFF FLAKE, Arizona
JO ANN DAVIS, Virginia
MIKE PENCE, Indiana
JOE WILSON, South Carolina
JOHN BOOZMAN, Arkansas
J. GRESHAM BARRETT, South Carolina
CONNIE MACK, Florida
JEFF FORTENBERRY, Nebraska
MICHAEL T. McCAUL, Texas
TED POE, Texas
BOB INGLIS, South Carolina
LUIS G. FORTUÑO, Puerto Rico
GUS BILIRAKIS, Florida

ROBERT R. KING, *Staff Director*
YLEEM POBLETE, *Republican Staff Director*

SUBCOMMITTEE ON AFRICA AND GLOBAL HEALTH

DONALD M. PAYNE, New Jersey, *Chairman*

DIANE E. WATSON, California
LYNN C. WOOLSEY, California
SHEILA JACKSON LEE, Texas
ADAM SMITH, Washington
BRAD MILLER, North Carolina

CHRISTOPHER H. SMITH, New Jersey
THOMAS G. TANCREDO, Colorado
JOHN BOOZMAN, Arkansas
JEFF FORTENBERRY, Nebraska
MICHAEL T. MCCAUL, Texas

NOELLE LUSANE, *Subcommittee Staff Director*
HEATHER FLYNN, *Subcommittee Professional Staff Member*
SHERI RICKERT, *Republican Professional Staff Member*
FAY JOHNSON, *Staff Associate*

(II)

CONTENTS

VULTURE FUNDS AND THE THREAT TO DEBT RELIEF IN AFRICA: A CALL TO ACTION AT THE G-8 AND BEYOND

THURSDAY, MAY 22, 2007

House of Representatives,
Subcommittee on Africa and Global Health,
Committee on Foreign Affairs,
Washington, DC.

The subcommittee met, pursuant to notice, at 2:34 p.m. in room 2172, Rayburn House Office Building, Hon. Donald M. Payne (chairman of the subcommittee) presiding.

Mr. PAYNE. The hearing will come to order.

Let me apologize for the lateness of the beginning of the hearing. We are going to actually have another vote in about 10 or 15 minutes. However, knowing the schedule of our witness, we will proceed to hear his statement, and then following his statement we will adjourn for a few minutes to have the rest of the testimony.

[The prepared statement of Mr. Payne follows:]

PREPARED STATEMENT OF THE HONORABLE DONALD M. PAYNE, A REPRESENTATIVE IN CONGRESS FROM THE STATE OF NEW JERSEY, AND CHAIRMAN, SUBCOMMITTEE ON AFRICA AND GLOBAL HEALTH

Good afternoon. Thank you all for joining the Subcommittee on Africa and Global Health for this very important hearing entitled: "Vulture Funds and the Threat to Debt Relief in Africa: A Call to Action at the G–8 and Beyond."

I learned about this new threat to the debt relief campaign in Africa this past February, as I was on my way to meet with President Ellen Johnson-Sirleaf of Liberia. Amy Goodman, host of the Pacifica Radio Show "Democracy Now" was speaking with BBC reporter Greg Palast on investigative reporting he had done on vulture funds. I was shocked to learn that Zambia, a southern African nation mired in poverty, was being sued by a US company Donegal International.

In 1979 Zambia borrowed agricultural equipment and services from Romania on credit. Zambia was unable to continue paying off the debt and made an agreement with Romania to liquidate the debt for $3.28 million. Before the deal was complete, Donegal International swooped in. Donegal International Limited is registered in the British Virgin Islands, but is an off-shoot of a Washington, D.C.-based company called Debt Advisory International, owned by a man named Michael Sheehan. Michael Sheehan sued Zambia in a UK court for $55 million. He purchased the debt for $3.28 million. The UK court recently ruled in favor of Donegal for $15 million. We will hear from our esteemed witnesses how this will hurt Zambia's development efforts.

That same day I heard the story on "Democracy Now," I met with President Bush, along with the Members of the Congressional Black Caucus. Mr. Conyers and I both mentioned our concerns with the vulture fund crisis. The President assured me his staff would look into it. And other nations are taking notice as well.

Top economic officials from the U.S., UK, Canada, France, Germany, Italy, Japan, and Russia—known collectively as the G8—will meet from June 6–8 in Germany. At the G8 summit German's Chancellor Angela Merkel and Prime Minister Tony Blair agreed to discuss vulture funds. Even the presumed next Prime Minister of

England, UK Chancellor of the Exchequer Gordon Brown has spoken out, saying recently, "I deplore the activities of the so-called vulture funds that seek to profit from debts owed by the poorest countries in the world. I am determined to limit the damage done by such funds."

The term "vulture fund" refers to a class of investors that operate in the secondary sovereign debt market known as distressed debt investors. They have been defined as "investment funds, particularly hedge funds and mutual funds, that purchase the debt of countries, or companies, that are in financial distress. These funds thus become creditors of the countries, or companies, through purchases of debt in the secondary market, rather than as primary lenders. "Vulture Funds" may seek to maximize their profit by buying below-market value debt prior to entering a restructuring negotiation, and then holding out in the negotiation in the hope of being paid full value, or by seeking to collect the full value of the debt through litigation. In addition to private securities, "vulture funds" have actively participated in the secondary sovereign debt market, a market with a $6 trillion annual turnover, according to the Congressional Research Service.

These funds feed upon financially distressed nations by purchasing their debt for pennies on the dollar only to turn around and demand through litigation the full value of the initial debt plus interest. Devoid of any moral compunction, these vulture funds take advantage of ambiguous international and domestic laws to collect on debts that were acquired by authoritarian regimes and that were not used in the legitimate interest of their people.

When world governments and international financial institutions created the Heavily Indebted Poor Countries (HIPC) Initiative and the Multilateral Debt Relief Initiative (MRDI) in 1996, indebted countries finally began to see a light at the end of the tunnel. Instead of servicing millions of dollars in debt annually, these nations could finally begin to service their own people. Schools could be built; teachers and nurses could be hired; life-saving medication could be distributed.

Yet, the threat of vulture funds waiting in the wings to swoop down and prey on struggling, impoverished nations in Africa, poverty reduction programs and plans for economic development could come to a grinding halt. These companies threaten to strip nations of the opportunity to apply newly freed financial resources towards achieving the UN Millennium Development Goals that improve quality of life for Africa's people. Meanwhile, these investors themselves stand to rake in millions upon millions of dollars off of African debt which they buy at a cheap price.

Thus, a few Americans are begetting fortunes at the expense of the misfortune and further impoverishment of millions of Africans. This is morally reprehensible and exploitative.

Very little is known about these companies that operate as vulture funds. They operate in the shadows where their actions are not monitored and their tactics change on a case-by-case basis. While the Zambian case brought this issue to the forefront for many of us, it is not unique. Over 20 HIPC countries have been the target of these funds since 1999 and approximately 40 more cases are on the horizon.

If something is not done to stem this tide, these funds could negate the efforts made by all the organizations engaged in debt relief, some of whom are represented today. Most importantly, vulture funds can undo the tremendous efforts made my HIPC countries who have worked to get their debt cancelled.

The Subcommittee on Africa and Global Health has been actively engaged in serious discussions with Chairman John Conyers' Judiciary committee and Chairman Barney Frank's Financial Services Committee, as these committees share jurisdiction over debt relief and a deep concern for the protection of heavily indebted nations. Chairman Conyers plans to hold a hearing in the near future and Chairman Frank is also studying the issue. It should be noted that this Congress will not turn a blind eye to the exploitative activities of Debt Advisory International or other US companies which prey on poor nations in Africa and elsewhere. We will continue to exercise oversight until we are satisfied that these nations are no longer at risk from these vulture funds.

For this hearing, we are honored to have Mr. Danny Glover who is not only a good friend whom I greatly admire, but is also a world-renowned Actor/Activist and Chairman of the Board of TransAfrica Forum. Mr Glover will testify on the first panel and will have to leave before 3:00 to catch a flight. We thank him for his strong interest, leadership on issues related to African nations, Haiti, and other important issues, and for his time today.

He will be followed by the second panel which will include Ms. Emira Woods, the Co-Director of Foreign Policy in Focus at the Institute of Policy Studies and Mr. Neil Watkins, Counsel for JubileeUSA. Emira Woods, a Liberian by birth, is well known in Washington and Africa for her commitment to debt relief in Africa and her work on Liberia. Neil Watkins has been working very closely on the vulture fund issue for Jublice, an organization which has championed the cause for poor nations to receive debt relief.

I would like to point out for the record that we contacted the Department of the Treasury to request Secretary Paulson or one of his deputies testify today. Unfortunately, he was unable to make it and Treasury said no one who was well-versed on the issue was available today due to the start of the US China Strategic Economic Dialogue which begins this week.

The BBC investigative reporter Greg Palast, who broke the story on Democracy Now with Amy Goodman, had planned to testify today but was unable at the last minute.

I thank the witnesses for their work and their time on this critical issue and look forward to their testimony.

With that, I turn to Ranking Member Chris Smith for opening remarks.

Mr. PAYNE. So let me just welcome you, Mr. Glover. It is always a pleasure to be with you. I will not take time to read your very outstanding background. Most of us know it. So it is a pleasure to be with you, and with that I will yield the time to you. Thank you very much for coming.

STATEMENT OF MR. DANNY GLOVER, CHAIRMAN OF THE BOARD, TRANSAFRICA FORUM, INC.

Mr. GLOVER. Thank you very much.

Mr. PAYNE. Now, push that little button in front of you on the microphone. There we go.

Mr. GLOVER. Thank you very much, Mr. Chairman, and also Representative Watson and Representative Woolsey. Thank you for inviting me to speak on the highly important issue of vulture funds.

I come today as the chairman of the board of TransAfrica Forum to address an issue that is at the forefront of our work. The primary goal of TransAfrica Forum is to promote progressive United States foreign policy toward Africa and diaspora, including the 150 million African descendants who are citizens of countries throughout this hemisphere.

For more than three decades, impoverished countries throughout Africa and Latin America have suffered under the massive crippling debt burden that has prevented sustainable growth, poverty alleviation, and economic development. Citizens in global society have fought tirelessly for debt relief and cancellation. Rich nations and the international financial institutions have begun debt relief regimes that have provided a chance for impoverished countries to start fresh and allocate desperately needed additional resources to health and education programs.

These debt relief mechanisms include the Highly Indebted Poor Countries Initiative, commonly known as HIPC, and the G–8 Multilateral Debt Relief Initiative, MDRI. Given the tremendous extent and scale of indebtedness of poor countries, we still have a long way to go to overhaul the international debt architecture and to tip the balance toward concrete sustainable development.

However, some progress has been made in relieving the debt crisis. In response to the global action and pressure, the United States under President Bush has also made a commitment to fight global hunger and to support debt relief. But as we advocate for debt relief, there are companies that seek to profit from it instead.

These vulture funds swoop in and seize the now freed resources, in the process destroying the benefits that international debt relief has offered. Vulture funds are companies and individuals who administer company business that buy the defaulted debt of highly indebted poor nations, and then seek repayment, often by suing these governments through courts in multiple jurisdictions, including the United States, for the full value of the debt plus interest, garnering much high paybacks.

The actions of these vulture funds often convert the benefits of international relief into private corporate gain, obstructing the process of securing debt relief for some countries and prohibiting others who have attained debt relief from investing their funds in much needed development. Through this privatization of national debt, increased misery is inflicted on the lives of millions of people across the developing world.

Since 1999, 20 HIPC countries have been threatened with or subject to legal actions by vulture funds. The indebted countries have almost always lost in the courtroom. Recently, vulture funds have targeted the country of Zambia, which qualified for G–8 debt cancellation in 2005. This is very significant because in Zambia over 70 percent of the population lives in poverty. The average wage is just over $1.00 a day. One in five people are infected with HIV/AIDS, and life expectancy has dropped to 37.7 years according to the 2006 UNDP Human Development Report.

But the nation was sued by Donegal International Limited, a private United States-owned company registered in the British Virgin Islands, for $55 million. This amount stands in stark contrast to the $3.28 million Donegal paid Romania for Zambia's debt.

In April of this year, the Royal Courts of Justice in London ordered the Zambian Government to pay Donegal $15.5 million. That means that Zambia will pay Donegal more than a third of what they received through the HIPC and the G–8 debt relief processes this year.

This vulture fund will strip Zambia of a sum of money that could have provided free education for over 150,000 children.

With firms like Donegal working hard to protect the business of the rich, how can civil society and the U.S. Government protect the children of the countries who will still face the devastation of vulture funds?

The morally bankrupt actions of vulture funds render the commitments of the debt relief made by the United States and other wealthy nations meaningless. We urge the international community to come up with an effective means to protect countries pursued by vulture funds in the future. At the coming G–8 summit, President Bush should call for commitments by world leaders to address vulture funds. These commitments could include international remedies preventing vulture funds from buying faulty debt and suing for repayment, and here in the United States Congress should pass legislation to prevent vulture funds from buying and collecting faulty debt.

Moreover, the international community must work together to put in place fair and transparent international debt resolution mechanisms while also creating an international financial architecture that promotes sustainable growth and takes cues from civil society.

In the short term, we urge the U.S. Government to assist countries currently facing legal action by providing them with free legal and financial advice. In addition, the U.S. Treasury should follow the example of the U.K. Chancellor Gordon Brown in pursuing means to limit the damage done by vulture funds.

As chairman of the board of TransAfrica Forum, I vow to work with our civil society partners and members of the committee to help create a legislative vehicle that can stop vulture funds from devouring African and Latin American economic progress.

Thank you very much sir.

[The prepared statement of Mr. Glover follows:]

PREPARED STATEMENT OF MR. DANNY GLOVER, CHAIRMAN OF THE BOARD, TRANSAFRICA FORUM, INC.

Good afternoon, Mr. Chairman, Representative Smith, distinguished members of the committee. Thank you for inviting me to speak on the highly important issue of Vulture Funds. I come today as the Chairman of the Board of TransAfrica Forum to address an issue that is at the forefront of our work. The primary goal of TransAfrica Forum is to promote progressive U.S. foreign policy towards Africa and the Diaspora, including the 150 million Afro-descendents who are citizens of countries throughout this hemisphere.

For more than three decades, impoverished countries throughout Africa and Latin America have suffered under a massive, crippling debt burden that has prevented sustainable growth, poverty alleviation, and economic development.

Citizens and global civil society have fought tirelessly for debt relief and cancellation. Rich nations and international financial institutions have begun debt relief regimes that have provided the chance for impoverished countries to start fresh and allocate desperately needed additional resources to health and education programs. These debt relief mechanisms include the Highly Indebted Poor Countries Initiatives, commonly known as HIPC, and the G8's Multi-lateral Debt Relief Initiative (MDRI). Given the tremendous extent and scale of indebtedness of poor countries, we still have a long way to go to overhaul the international debt architecture and to tip the balance towards concrete, sustainable development. However, some progress has been made in relieving the debt crisis.

In response to global action and pressure, the United States, under President Bush, has also made a commitment to fight global hunger and to support debt relief. But as we advocate for debt relief, there are companies that seek to profit from it instead. These Vulture Funds swoop in and seize the now freed resources, in the process destroying the benefits that international debt relief has offered. Vulture Funds are companies, and individuals who administer company business, that buy the defaulted debt of highly-indebted poor nations and then seek repayment, often by suing these governments through courts in multiple jurisdictions, including the United States, for the full value of the debt plus interest, garnering much higher paybacks. The actions of these Vulture Funds often convert the benefits of international debt relief into private corporate gain-obstructing the process of securing debt relief for some countries and prohibiting others who have attained debt relief from investing those funds in much-needed development. Through this privatization of national debt, increased misery is inflicted on the lives of millions of people across the developing world.

Since 1999, 20 HIPC Countries have been threatened with or subject to legal actions by Vulture Funds. The indebted countries have almost always lost in the courtroom. Recently, Vulture Funds have targeted the country of Zambia, which qualified for G8 debt cancellation in 2005. This is very significant because in Zambia over 70% of the population lives in poverty; the average wage is just over a dollar a day; one in five people are infected with HIV/AIDS; and life expectancy has dropped to 37.7 years, according to the 2006 UNDP Human Development Report. But the nation was sued by Donegal International Ltd., a private U.S.-owned company registered in the British Virgin Islands, for $55 million. This amount stands in stark contrast to the $3.28 million Donegal paid Romania for Zambia's debt. In April this year, The Royal Courts of Justice in London ordered that Zambia pay Donegal $15.5 million. That means that Zambia will pay Donegal more than a third of what they received through the HIPC and G8 debt relief processes this year. This Vulture Fund will strip Zambia of a sum of money that could have provided free education for over 150,000 children.

With firms like Donegal working hard to protect the business of the rich, how can civil society and the U.S. government protect the children of the countries who will still face the devastation of Vulture Funds?

The morally bankrupt actions of Vulture Funds render the commitments to debt relief made by the United States and other wealthy nations meaningless. We urge the international community to come up with effective means to protect countries pursued by Vulture Funds in the future.

At the upcoming G8 Summit, President Bush should call for commitments by world leaders to address Vulture Funds. These commitments could include international remedies preventing Vulture Funds from buying faulty debt and suing for repayment. And here in the United States, Congress should pass legislation to prevent Vulture Funds from buying and collecting faulty debt.

Moreover, the international community must work together to put into place fair and transparent international debt resolution mechanisms, while also creating an international financial architecture that promotes sustainable growth and takes cues from civil society.

In the short term, we urge the U.S. government to assist countries currently facing legal action by providing them with free legal and financial advice. In addition, the U.S. Treasury should follow the example of U.K. Chancellor Gordon Brown in pursuing means to limit the damage done by Vulture Funds.

As Chairman of the Board of TransAfrica Forum, I vow to work with our civil society partners and Members of this committee to help create a legislative vehicle that can stop Vulture Funds from devouring African and Latin American economic progress.

Mr. PAYNE. Well, let me thank you very much for that powerful presentation, and we will look forward to working with you and TransAfrica and the other groups that have a concern about this issue. I will raise the point, as I mentioned when we return, to President Bush the morning that I heard it on——

Mr. GLOVER. Democracy Now?

Mr. PAYNE [continuing]. And so we will definitely be dealing with this. I know you have to catch a plane, but I would once again like to thank you. Normally we would ask you a question or two but we are going to let you run. We have a vote that is coming up in about 3 or 4 minutes, so we will have to leave too.

So we will adjourn and we will be back following this next vote, and thank you very much. It is good to see you again, sir.

Mr. GLOVER. Good to see you. Good to see you.

Mr. PAYNE. Thank you.

[Recess.]

Mr. PAYNE. Good afternoon. Once again we apologize for the delays but they are unpredictable. Let me welcome all of you here again this afternoon, and to my colleague, Ms. Woolsey and to Congresswoman Watson, who was here earlier and may return. I am not sure.

Let me thank all of you for joining the Subcommittee on Africa and Global Health. It is a very important hearing entitled "Vulture Funds and the Treat to Debt Relief in Africa: A Call to Action at the G–8 and Beyond." We certainly were very pleased that Mr. Glover was able to give his testimony, and he has done so many great things working for the underserved, whether it is in the Caribbean or South America, Haiti, or Africa. If we had more people like that in the entertainment field, I think many of our issues would be highlighted since people do listen to some of our outstanding Americans. So I certainly appreciated his participation.

When world governments and international financial institutions create the Heavily Indebted Poor Countries, the HIPC, and the Multilateral Debt Relief Initiative, MDRI mentioned by Mr. Glover, in 1996, indebted countries finally began to see a light at the end of the tunnel. They would be released from the billions of dollars in debt they had incurred, many through previous dictators and questionable contracts with Western nations.

Instead of servicing millions of dollars in debt annually, these nations could finally begin to service their own people. Schools could be built. Teachers and nurses could be hired. Life-saving medications could be distributed.

Since then great advances have been made toward canceling Africa's debt, yet there are new threats, so-called vulture funds waiting in the wings to swoop down and prey on struggling impoverished nations in Africa, as we have heard from our previous speaker. Now poverty-reduction programs and plans for economic development could come to a grinding halt. These companies threaten to strip nations of opportunities to apply newly-found financial resources toward achieving the U.N. millennium development goals that improve the quality of life for African people, meanwhile, these investors themselves stand to rack in millions upon millions of dollars off the African debt, which they buy at a very cheap price.

The term "vulture fund" refers to a class of investors that operate on a secondary sovereign debt market known as "distressed debt investors." They have been defined as investment funds, particularly hedge funds, and mutual funds that purchase the debt of countries or companies that are in financial distress. Vulture funds seek to maximize their profit by buying below market value debt prior to entering a restructuring negotiation, and then holding out the negotiations in hope of being paid full value, plus interest and fees through litigation.

The secondary sovereign debt market in which vulture funds have actively participated in is a market with $6 trillion annual turnover, according to the Congressional Research Service. Vulture funds feed upon financially distressed nations by purchasing their debt for pennies on the dollar, only to turn around and demand through litigation the full value of the initial debt, plus interest.

Devoid of any moral compunction, these vulture funds take advantage of ambiguous international and domestic laws to collect on debts that were acquired by authoritarian regimes that were not used in legitimate interests of the people. Thus, a few Americans are getting fortunes at the expense and the misfortune and further impoverishment of millions of Africans. This is morally reprehensible, and exploitative.

A year ago I heard about the vulture funds in Congo-Brazzaville. This past February I heard about the issue again as I was on my way to meet with President Ellen Johnson-Sirleaf of Liberia. Amy Goldman, host of Pacifica Radio Show "Democracy Now," was interviewing BBC Reporter Greg Palast on investigative reporting he had done on the issue.

On my way listening in the car, I was just shocked by what I heard. I learned about the Zambia situation as we all know and also referred to by Mr. Glover. A southern African nation marred in poverty was being used by a United States company, the Donegal International Fund.

In 1979, Zambia borrowed agricultural equipment and services from Romania on credit. Zambia was unable to continue paying off the debt and made an agreement with Romania to liquidate the debt for $3.28 million. Before the debt was complete, Donegal International swooped in. Donegal International Limited is registered in the British Virgin Islands, but is an off-shoot of a Washington, DC-based company called Debt Advisory International, owned by a man named Michael Sheehan.

Michael Sheehan sued Zambia in a U.K. court for $55 million. He purchased the debt for $3.2 million. The U.K. court recently ruled in favor of Donegal for $15 million. We will hear from our esteemed witnesses how this will hurt Zambia's development efforts.

While the Zambian case brought this issue to the forefront for many of us, it is not unique. Over 20 HIPC countries have been the target of these funds since 1999, and approximately 40 more cases are on the horizon coming up in the future.

The same day I heard the story on Democracy Now, I met with President Bush, along with members of the Congressional Black Caucus. Mr. Conyers and I both mentioned our concern with vulture funds and the crisis that it is creating. The President assured me and his staff that he would look into the matter, and although other nations are taking notice as well, immediate action must be taken as soon as possible.

Top economic officials from the United States, U.K., Canada, France, Germany, Italy, Japan, and Russia, known collectively as we know as the G–8, will meet from June 6 to 8 in Germany. During the G–8 summit, German's Chancellor Angela Merkel and Prime Minister Tony Blair agreed to discuss vulture funds at that upcoming summit. Even the presumed next prime minister of England, U.K. Chancellor of the Exchequer Gordon Brown has spoken out, saying recently, "I deplore the activities of the so-called vulture funds that seek to profit from debts owed by the poorest countries in the world. I am determined to limit the damage done by such funds."

If something is not done to stem the tide, these funds could undermine the effort made by an organization engaged in debt relief, some of whom are represented here today. Most importantly, vulture funds can undue the tremendous efforts made by HIPC countries who have worked to get their debt canceled.

The Subcommittee on Africa and Global Health has been actively engaged in serious discussion with Chairman John Conyers of the Judiciary Committee and Chairman Barney Frank of the Financial Services Committee, as these committees share jurisdiction over debt relief, and a deep concern for the protection of heavily indebted nations. Chairman Conyers is planning to have a meeting in the near future and Chairman Frank is also studying the issue.

It should be noted that this Congress will not turn a blind eye to the exploitive activities of Debt Advisory International or other United States companies which prey on poor nations in Africa and elsewhere, and other companies from wherever they are in the world. We will continue to exercise oversight until we are satisfied that these nations are no longer at risk from these venture funds.

We were very pleased to hear from Danny Glover and we will not move to our panel. We have with us, who will be on this panel, Ms.

Emira Woods who is the co-director of Foreign Policy in Focus at the Institute for Policy Studies. She has done a tremendous amount of work and holds a B.A. in international relations from Columbia, certified public policy from Woodrow Wilson School at Princeton, a master's in government from Harvard, an ABD in political economy and government at Harvard, and has been very active with the USAID and Treasury programs. She is very well prepared and equipped to be one of our witnesses.

I guess probably most importantly, *Essence* said she is a "Woman who is shaping the world," so I guess that might be the—if *Essence* said it, it is really something.

Secondly, we have with us Mr. Neil Watkins who is a national coordinator for Jubilee USA Network, and he has been working on debt cancellation for a number of years. As we may know, Jubilee USA is an alliance of more than 80 religious denominations, faith-based networks, development agencies, labor, environment and community organizations working to generate the political will for cancellation of unjust debt in Africa, Asia, and Latin America.

He has been very active. He graduated from Georgetown University School of Foreign Service, and has spent a year working in Dakar, Senegal, wherein he focused his studies in college on African studies.

So it is a pleasure to have both of you, and we will start with Ms. Woods.

STATEMENT OF MS. EMIRA WOODS, M.A., ABD, CO–DIRECTOR FOR FOREIGN POLICY IN FOCUS, INSTITUTE FOR POLICY STUDIES

Ms. WOODS. Thank you, Chairman Payne and Congresswoman Woolsey, for your leadership on this issue, for convening this hearing today. I am here representing the Institute for Policy Studies, an institute that has a 40-year history of research and action for peace, justice and the environment, and we really want to thank you for the leadership that you are showing today and for the leadership that you have shown consistently when it comes to Africa.

We know that it is this bold leadership that well over 10 years ago now made a decision that poor people in poor nations deserve debt relief. It is your leadership from Congress, with the administration, that actually led to the creation of a debt relief system now known as the Heavily Indebted Poor Country Initiative, and it is initiatives like this that have lifted the burden off of many countries throughout the world.

Yet we also know that today in Zambia and several other countries a new set of rich actors is actually undermining the moral promise made for debt relief almost a decade ago. These vulture funds are violating the promise of debt relief as they enrich themselves, and we are basically here today to say this is absolutely an outrage.

In this testimony, I am going to concentrate really on Zambia and Liberia. I was happy to hear you talk about your meeting with Ellen Johnson-Sirleaf because we recognize that Zambia is the case in front of us today, but Liberia could well be the case in front of us tomorrow. We will start with Zambia.

Zambia, as you well know, Congressman Payne, is a poor, land-locked country in southern Africa. The main source of income for Zambia is copper. But in the mid-seventies the price of copper, like many other commodities, plummeted. This decline in commodity prices actually forced countries like Zambia to turn to the international community, especially the international financial institutions, to actually help to keep things going, to keep their economies afloat.

This, together with increasing interest rates in the 1980s, led to a sky-rocketing debt for Zambia. The Zambia remains one of the most highly indebted countries today.

We know also that Zambia, according to the U.N. Human Development Index, is 166 out of 175 of the world's poorest countries. Sixty-eight percent of Zambia's 11 million people live on less than $1.00 a day. Zambians throughout the country are really plagued with inadequate schooling, housing, health care, the list is long. But we recognize that thanks to the leadership of Congress and the administration, listening to the voices of civil society around the world, the Zambia from 2000 on celebrated debt reduction.

We are honored really to be working with one of the groups in Zambia, Jubilee Zambia, and I would love to read a quote from one of our colleagues there, Charity Musamba, who said:

"With debt relief, even in spite of debt relief, we still have obligations to continue servicing our debt, and every year from the little resources we have and from the little revenue that we earn we still have to service our debt. With these monies that we are paying in debt service, we can provide better water facilities for certain communities, we can help vulnerable children, we could use this amount of money to support elderly parents who are looking after orphans, particularly with HIV/AIDS rate escalating. There is a lot we could do with this money, but because we are obliged to pay it back, our government has no choice."

Charity went on to explain how conditions imposed in return for debt relief have included a freeze on the wages of government employees, including teaches and nurses. Thanking debt campaigners, Charity asked us all to keep focused on the prize. She recognized that Zambia courageously committed funds for debt relief to building schools and sustaining hospitals. Yet we also recognize that those steps forward are very much in jeopardy today.

As you said already in your opening statement, we know that in late April a U.K. court ruled that Zambia must pay Donegal International, a vulture fund, officially located in the British Virgins Islands, but mostly owned by Debt Advisory International, $15 million for debt acquired for just over $3 million from the Romanian Government.

Donegal, as we well know, is a vulture firm based right here in Washington, DC, and led by an American investor, Michael Sheehan. This year Zambia expects to save $40 million from debt relief. Paying Donegal $15 million would severely limit the relief's impact.

As a result of the egregious behavior of these debt vulture funds, Zambian children will continue to stay out of school, and infants will continue to die from curable diseases. The $15 million award is approximately three-quarters of the funds allocated for the recruitment of new teachers in Zambia in 2007 alone. Payment of this unjust claim will certainly derail Zambia's achievement of the millennium development goals.

One main lesson from the Zambian case is that while debt negotiations are confidential and not publicly available, it opens up current and future generations to speculators and other corrupt practices. We firmly believe that it is immoral for Donegal to ask for a profit of several million dollars over and above the price it paid for the Zambia's debt.

Moreover, debt repayments to Donegal International will upset Zambia's fiscal stability and ability to deliver public services. Mr. Sheehan and his agents did not act honestly in the acquisition of the debt, and we recognize that the purchase of the debt undermines and erodes the benefits of the debt relief mechanisms, both in HIPC, the Heavily Indebted Poor Country Imitative, and in the Multilateral Debt Relief Initiative.

So we are worried about the Zambia and the impacts of this case on ordinary peoples' lives.

But it is not just Zambia, as you said in your opening statement. There are over 27 countries, almost half the African continent, that are currently facing similar circumstances as Zambia, and we recognize that in terms of future cases there could be at least 40 countries facing a similar circumstance.

So let me begin with Liberia. I am from Liberia and that probably comes the easiest, and we recognize that Liberia's 26-year descent into chaos started in the 1980s when the Reagan administration funneled military hardware, training, and finances to the regime of the ruthless dictator, Samuel Doe. Under Doe's watch, American military aid to Liberia, often in the form of loans, increased 10-fold. Doe also racked up enormous debts as he and his cronies stole elections and built their machinery of repression. This aid actually led to the death of 250,000 Liberians, and yet now it is on the backs of the citizens of Liberia and Africa's first woman President to repay a debt that has ballooned from the 1980s to a rate of $4 billion today.

Liberia is currently repaying those debts at a monthly rate of $60,000, which doesn't really seem like much, but in Liberia's situation it is the equivalent of six hospitals or clinics that could have been built in the first year of the Ellen Johnson administration.

As the political will mounted for Liberia's debt cancellation, the vultures started to swoop. We recognize that, according to Liberia's Ministry of Finance, of Liberia's $4 billion debt and estimated $1.5 billion, $1.5 billion with a "b" is owned by these hedge funds. This opens up Liberia as it is beginning to emerge out of its 26th-year chaos to incredible volatility, both economically and politically.

We are shocked at the scale of this situation in Liberia, and we are concerned that Liberia, as well as the other countries that make up the 40 about to face these legal cases, are in grave danger.

So what are our ideas? Our ideas are many and we are going to share them together with Jubilee. The first is recognizing that in advancing the debt initiative, HIPC, Highly Indebted Poor Country Initiate, we left out key things.

We left out recognition of the onerous conditions being placed on debtor countries, and we also left out any kind of recognition of commercial debt, the debt that is being now harped on by these vultures. We have to reexamine the Heavily Indebted Poor Country Initiative, and we ask as a first step this committee to consider instructions to U.S. Treasury for the revamping of HIPC.

Second, we recognize that we need internationally-binding, legal constraints on the operations of these vulture funds. Congress should take all possible legal measures to prevent such predatory litigation and to ensure that it does not undermine international debt relief initiatives or restructuring mechanisms.

Congress should also work to apply legal constraints, and if needed, prosecute fully all aspects of corrupt practices linked to such cases. We urge this committee to instruct Treasury to negotiate an international mechanism that will bring a fair and transparent process for creditors and debtors to responsibly reduce the debt burden on developing countries.

But we also know the third step is critically important, and that step is canceling all odious and illegitimate debt. We recognize that the debt of countries like Liberia, dictator debt really, is illegitimate and odious and we urge efforts be made to acknowledge the illegitimacy of those debts as it has been acknowledged in instances like Iraq, and to move steadfastly for the cancellation of all odious debt so that countries are not further hampered by this debt burden, opening up opportunities for vultures to swoop in.

We thank you for your leadership on this issue. We look forward to your questions and to sustained engagement with you as we look to stemming this problem and making sure that we do not have a steady flow of other countries facing a similar circumstance. Thank you.

[The prepared statement of Ms. Woods follows:]

PREPARED STATEMENT OF MS. EMIRA WOODS, M.A., ABD, CO-DIRECTOR FOR FOREIGN POLICY IN FOCUS, INSTITUTE FOR POLICY STUDIES

"In a world of plenty, poverty can and must be eliminated by changing the structural imbalances that create and maintain impoverishment in Africa and around the world." African economist, Samir Amin

Chairman Payne, Ranking Member Smith, distinguished members of the House Committee on Foreign Affairs, Subcommittee on Africa and Global Health, I would like to thank you for your invitation to participate in this hearing on "Vulture Funds and the Threat to Debt Relief in Africa: A Call to Action at the G–8 and Beyond."

The Congress of the United States and the president of the United States took a huge step forward about 10 years ago when they stated that yes, it was a moral imperative to give poor people in poor nations debt relief. Political leaders, including those in Congress, stated emphatically that it was simply wrong that poor people be burdened with repaying debts incurred by rich leaders. Yet, today, in Zambia and several other countries, a new set of rich actors is undermining that moral promise. These "vulture funds" are violating that promise of debt relief as they enrich themselves. This is an outrage.

In this testimony, I will present my deep concerns with the expansion of vulture funds and offer some solutions to this growing problem.

I. IMPACT OF VULTURE FUNDS ON AFRICA

The story of debt in Africa begins in the 1960s and it is not a pretty story. In many countries, undemocratic governments (in many cases, outright dictatorships)

began borrowing large amounts of money from both official sources (governments and multilateral institutions and from banks and other private sources. Much of this money went into boondoggles that massaged the egos of the dictators, some of it went into private bank accounts and small amounts of it went into real projects that benefited Africans.

The debt crisis emerged in the 1980s when interest rates rose to epic proportions, and commodity prices were low, and country after country experienced difficulties in repaying the debts. At this stage, the creditors invariably sent in the International Monetary Fund to press for countries to shift policies towards exports, toward privatization, all with the goal of getting the loans repaid. The poor and the environment paid a heavy price.

Happily, by the late 1990s, Under pressure from groups in the South and North, governments agreed that much of this debt should be cancelled. And, governments at the G–8 meetings and elsewhere devised a HIPC that would carry out the debt relief. However, there were two big problems with HIPC:

- onerous conditions;
- no one foresaw the vulture fund problem.

So, today, there is very little meaningful debt cancellation and every African nation is vulnerable to vulture funds.

II. IMPACT OF VULTURE FUNDS ON ZAMBIA AND LIBERIA

My testimony will focus on two countries. One, Zambia, has already faced the ravishes of vulture funds in legal proceedings. The other, Liberia, may be one of the forthcoming cases in the not too distant future.

Zambia

Zambia is a poor land-locked country in Southern Africa whose main source of external income is copper. In the mid-1970s, the price of copper suffered a severe decline worldwide. Zambia turned to foreign and international lenders for relief, but, as copper prices remained depressed, it became increasingly difficult to service its growing debt. By the mid-1990s, despite limited debt relief, Zambia's per capita foreign debt remained among the highest in the world.

Today, the United Nations Human Development Index ranks Zambia 166 out of 175 of the poorest countries. Sixty-eight percent of Zambia's 11 million people live on less than a dollar a day. Zambians throughout the country are plagued by inadequate schools, housing, healthcare. In 2000, Zambia was one of the countries spotlighted by an international campaign for debt relief.

According to Charity Musamba of Jubilee Zambia:

Even after the year 2000, with debt relief, we still have the obligation to continue servicing debt. And every year, from the little resources that we have, from the little revenue that we earn from [exports] we still have to service our debts. And the cost per year ranges from about £80 to £135 million per year. "This figure looks very small as I'm standing in England. But I can assure you, from the point of view of Zambia, we can provide better water facilities for certain communities using the money. We can also help the vulnerable children using this amount of money . . . We could use this amount of money to support those elderly parents who are looking after orphans. There's a lot that we could use this money for. But because we are obliged to pay back, our government has no choice.

Charity went on to explain how conditions imposed in return for debt relief have included a freeze on the wages of government employees, including teachers and nurses, all of whom are denied a living wage. But she also spoke of the benefits that limited debt cancellation has had so far, thanking debt campaigners, and asking them to keep up the work. Zambia has courageously committed funds from debt relief to building and sustaining schools and hospitals.

In late April, a UK court ruled that Zambia must pay Donegal International, a vulture fund officially located in the British Virgin Islands but mostly owned by Debt Advisory International, $15 million for debt acquired for just over $3 million from the Romanian government. Donegal is a secretive firm based in Washington DC and led by American investor Michael Sheehan. This year, Zambia expects to save $40 million from debt relief. Paying Donegal $15 million would severely limit the relief's impact.

As a result of the egregious behavior of debt vulture funds, Zambian children will continue to stay out of school and infants will continue to die from curable diseases. The $15.5 million award is approximately three quarters of the funds allocated for recruitment of new teachers in Zambia's 2007 national budget for Zambia. Payment of this unjust claim will certainly derail Zambia's achievement of the Millennium Development Goals (MDGs).

One main lesson from the Zambian case is that where debt negotiations are "confidential and not publicly available" (language from Justice Smith's judgment) it opens up future generations to speculators and other corrupt corporate practices.

Probably the hardest lesson is that the Zambian people will have to suffer at the hands of past dishonest activities of irresponsible leaders and present vulture greed of private investors.

- It is immoral for Donegal to ask for a profit of several millions dollars (US$ 55 million) over and above the price (US$ 3.3 million) it paid for the Zambian debt.
- Debt repayments to Donegal International will upset Zambia's fiscal stability and ability to deliver public services.
- Mr. Sheehan and his agents did not act very honestly in the acquisition of this debt as noted by Judge Smith of the London court.
- The purchase of the debt undermines and erodes the full intended benefits from debt relief arrangements initiated through the Highly Indebted Poor Country Initiative (HIPC) and the Multi-lateral Debt Relief Initiative (MDRI).

Liberia

Liberia's 26-year descent into chaos started in the 1980s when the Reagan Administration funneled military hardware, training, and finances to the regime of the ruthless dictator Samuel Doe. Under Doe's watch, American military aid to Liberia, often in the form of loans, increased ten-fold. Doe also racked up enormous debts as his cronies stole elections and built their machinery of repression. This military "aid" built the machinery of repression that led to the deaths of an estimated 250,000 Liberians. Much of the "assistance" in the 1980's came in the form of loans, which have now ballooned to push Liberia's debt burden to over $4 billion The Liberian people and the government of Africa's first woman president are now being asked to foot the bill.

Liberia pays $60,000 each month in debt service payment. This is the equivalent of six hospitals or clinics that could have been built in the first year of the Ellen Johnson Sirleaf Administration. As the political will mounted for Liberia's debt cancellation, the vultures started their deadly hover. While an estimated 44 countries have debt owed to vulture funds, by virtue of its size and complexity, Liberia could be the most dramatic case of all when compared with per capita income. According to Liberia's Ministry of Finance, Totaling one-third of outstanding debt, Liberia's commercial debt, a full $1.5 billion is now owned by hedge funds. It may well be only a matter of time before the vultures pursue their "claims" in court, which would be a devastating blow for the new government.

III. THREE IDEAS ON REINING IN THE NEGATIVE IMPACT OF VULTURE FUNDS

A. Fixing Flawed Debt "Relief"

The "vultures attack on African countries is due in part to the flawed mechanism established in 1996 to deal with developing country debt, the Heavily Indebted Poor Countries (HIPC) initiative of the international financial institutions. The HIPC initiative was poorly funded, ill conceived, and left a big loophole by not addressing commercial debt.

Not only has the HIPC initiative not lifted the debt burden, but it has also imposed onerous constraints that have held back the continent's growth and progress. Under the guise of debt relief, the U.S. Treasury and the international institutions found a way to impose multinational corporations on Africa's water, electricity, education and health systems, bringing higher fees and even further impoverishment to the region.

In a 2004 report, the World Development Movement Report notes "The evidence suggests that the past twenty years of IMF and World Bank intervention have exacerbated rather than ameliorated Zambia's debt crisis. Ironically, in return for debt relief, Zambia is required to do more of the same. The country has been condemned to debt." Now is the time to examine critically the factors contributing to debt and the downward pressure on African economies.

Revamping HIPC is a critical step in address the root issues of Africa's debt problems.

B) Establish internationally binding legal constraints on the operations of vulture funds that prey on impoverished countries like Zambia

Congress should take all possible legal measures to prevent such predatory litigation and to ensure that it does not undermine international debt relief initiatives or restructuring mechanisms. Congress should also work to apply legal constraints and if needed prosecute fully all aspects of corrupt practices linked to such cases.

I urge the committee to instruct Treasury to negotiate an international mechanism that will bring a fair and transparent process for creditors and debtors to responsibly reduce the debt burden on developing countries.

C) Cancel Odious Debt—Africa has already paid enough

The UN Conference on Trade and Development (UNCTAD), in a comprehensive report on debt sustainability, noted that between 1970 and 2002, sub-Saharan Africa received $294 billion in disbursements, paid out $268 billion in debt service and yet remained straddled with a debt stock of some $210 billion. The average African country spends three times more of its scarce resources on repaying debt than it does on providing basic services. This daily transfer siphons off scarce resources needed to address the HIV/AIDS pandemic and other key concerns of the continent. In fact, African nations are still paying more in debt service to the United States and other creditors than they receive in aid, new loans, or investment. In addressing Africa's struggle for relief from its onerous external debt, advocates of global justice have raised a critical question: Who owes whom?

What is needed is acknowledgement and cancellation of all odious Debt.

Under the legal principle of odious debt, debts are regarded as illegitimate when the creditor is aware that loans to governments are made without the consent of the people and not spent in their interests. The U.S. was the first to use this doctrine. After conquering Cuba in 1898, it repudiated Cuban debts to former colonial power Spain because the loans never had the consent of the people. More recently, the Bush Administration has used the same argument for Iraq. Africa's odious debt, Liberia the debt incurred by Liberia's dictator Samuel Doe needs comprehensive and complete cancellation, with no onerous conditions.

Thank you for convening this hearing and for your leadership on this critical issue. I look forward to your questions.

Mr. PAYNE. Thank you very much for that very powerful testimony.

Mr. Watkins.

STATEMENT OF MR. NEIL WATKINS, NATIONAL COORDINATOR, JUBILEE USA NETWORK

Mr. WATKINS. Thank you. Chairman Payne, Representative Woolsey, Representative Jackson Lee, and members of the committee, I would like to thank you for the invitation to offer testimony today.

Jubilee USA Network is grateful for the committee's leadership on this issue, and for looking at the real challenge brought by vulture funds in Africa.

With the help of Congress, we have made significant steps in addressing the crisis of unjust debt over the past few years, but these advances are threatened by these vulture funds. In response to the Jubilee 2000 campaign in the late 1990s, the G–8 made commitments in 1999, and again in 2005 to provide debt cancellation to nations in Africa and Latin America. Today, 18 African nations have benefitted from 100 percent debt cancellation of their IMF and World Bank debts.

Resources released by debt relief to date are reaching the poor. Uganda used its $57.9 million savings last year on primary education, malaria control, health care, and infrastructure to expand access to water and electricity. Zambia used its savings of more than $23 million last year to eliminate fees for health care in rural areas.

I had the opportunity to go to Zambia in January with a delegation of about a dozen Jubilee supporters and we saw firsthand the impact of this policy. We saw a health clinic in a rural area of Zambia called Siavanga where previously people had to pay fees to get access to care. Those fees are now gone thanks to debt relief.

But while limited progress has been made on debt, there is a significant unfinished agenda. 2007 is the Sabbath year. It is a year when in the Bible debts were also canceled as in the jubilee year. In this Sabbath year, Jubilee USA is working to address the unfinished agenda on debt by calling for debt cancellation for more countries, for an end to harmful economic conditions, for an audit of odious and illegitimate lending, and for an end to the practice of vulture funds and other creditors which are profiting from debt cancellation granted by the U.S. Government and the G–8.

Now, vulture funds are not a new phenomenon. In the late 1990s, Elliott Associates successfully sued the Government of Peru, a middle income country, and won $55 million. But now that heavily indebted poor countries, or HIPC nations, have received debt cancellation, vulture funds are beginning to target them as well. Suddenly these nations have more access to cash freed up by debt cancellation, and thus they look more attractive to opportunistic vulture funds.

It is important to note that vulture funds are not the only creditors that are taking advantage of or "free riding" on debt relief. Other creditors, including non-Paris Club official creditors, smaller, multilateral creditors, and quasi-commercial lenders must also be addressed and encouraged to cancel their claims on indebted countries.

As other witnesses have mentioned, a number of these creditors are suing African countries, and a number of these legal actions have taken place since 1999. What is common to all of these cases is that the debtor governments almost always lose.

Consider the human impact of these lawsuits. In Niger, the government spent more than half of what it spent on health and education in 1 year combined on lawsuits brought by commercial creditors. At this very moment countries like Liberia, as Emira mentioned, Cameroon, the Republic of Congo, and others, are facing suits or threats of litigation from vulture funds. Action is needed now so that what happened to Zambia will not happen again to other African nations.

More than two-thirds of lawsuits brought against indebted countries by vulture funds and other commercial creditors occur in the United States or the United Kingdom. The United States must be a leader in addressing this problem.

So how should the G–8 and Congress address this issue? In recent weeks, the Bush administration, the U.K. Government, and the German Government, and the G–8 finance ministers meeting last weekend have all publicly stated concern about the threat posed by vulture funds. These statements of concern are welcome, but they must now be followed by strong action at the upcoming G–8 summit to be held in Germany just under 2 weeks from now, from June 6 to 8.

Congress can play a critical role by encouraging the administration to support specific policy proposals to address the challenge presented by vulture funds. Specifically, we are asking for Congress's support and calling on the Bush administration and the G–8 leaders to, first, urge the World Bank to more aggressively buy back outstanding commercial debts in eligible countries. This would get debts at risk of being bought up by vulture funds out of the public domain so that the vultures cannot strike again. The World Bank could expand its IDA debt reduction facility to be available to pre-decision point countries like Liberia, and to allow countries that have already used the fund to use it again.

Second, we are calling on the G–8 and the Bush administration to support the development of strong codes of conduct for commercial creditors and a charter for responsible lending.

Third, we should increase technical and legal assistance to countries with debts at risk of being sued by vulture funds. This support should be extended to prevent lawsuits from being brought against governments and to help once there is a suit that is brought.

These three proposals can be quickly implemented with the support of the G–8, Congress, and international financial institutions, and should help slow the pace of lawsuits.

A soon to be introduced piece of legislation, the Jubilee Act for Responsible Lending and Expanded Debt Cancellation, will also include several provisions to reduce vulture activity. This is one specific legislative proposal that members can support while legislation more focused on vulture funds is in development.

Beyond these steps, Congress should pursue changes in U.S. law which would forbid profiteering by vulture funds in the future.

To conclude, vulture funds undermine the effectiveness of debt cancellation. Action should be taken now to ensure that the gains from debt cancellation are preserved.

Thank you.

[The prepared statement of Mr. Watkins follows:]

PREPARED STATEMENT OF MR. NEIL WATKINS, NATIONAL COORDINATOR, JUBILEE USA NETWORK

I'd like to thank Chairman Payne, Ranking Member Smith, and members of the committee for the invitation to share this testimony today. I come before you today as a representative of Jubilee USA Network. Jubilee USA is an alliance of more than 80 religious denominations, faith-based networks, development agencies, and labor, environment and community organizations working to generate the political will for cancellation of unjust debts in Africa, Asia, and Latin America. Founded in 1997, the Network is the US arm of the global Jubilee debt cancellation movement.

We are grateful for the committee's leadership in addressing the critical challenge posed by so-called "vulture funds" to heavily indebted poor nations, especially in Africa.

DEBT CANCELLATION: A TOOL TO FIGHT POVERTY

Impoverished countries in Africa have been struggling under the crushing burden of international debts for many years, dating to the 1970s. In the late 1990s, Jubilee campaigners across the globe united to bring attention to the debt crisis at an international level; this pressure led to concrete commitments from G–8 leaders and the international financial institutions to provide limited debt cancellation for some of the world's poorest nations.

Since 1996, when the Heavily Indebted Poor Countries Initiative (HIPC) was created, more than 30 nations have seen some form of debt relief. Congress has demonstrated its support for bilateral and multilateral debt relief through the enactment of comprehensive debt relief initiatives for heavily indebted low-income countries.

In 2005, the United States and other G–8 nations reached an agreement to provide 100% debt cancellation of debts owed by eligible poor nations to Paris Club members, the IMF, the World Bank, and the African Development Bank. The 2005 agreement led to the creation of the Multilateral Debt Relief Initiative (MDRI). As of April 2007, 22 nations, including 18 in Africa, have seen the majority of their debts to the IMF, World Bank, and African Development Bank cancelled under the terms of the MDRI.

Resources released by debt relief efforts to date are reaching the poor. Cameroon is using the US $29.8 million of savings it will gain from the MDRI in 2006 for national poverty reduction priorities, including infrastructure, social sector and governance reforms. Uganda is using its US $57.9 million savings in 2006 on improving energy infrastructure to try to ease acute electricity shortages, as well as primary education, malaria control, healthcare and water infrastructure (specifically targeting the poor and under-served villages). Zambia is using its savings of US $23.8 million under the MDRI in 2006 to increase spending on agricultural projects on smallholder irrigation and livestock disease control, as well as to eliminate fees for healthcare in rural areas.

While debt cancellation has a record of success, there remains an unfinished agenda on international debt. There are a number of challenges to the effective implementation of existing commitments, and broader cancellation of unfair and unjust debts is needed if the global community is to reach the Millennium Development Goals. One of those challenges is the threat posed by vulture funds.

VULTURE FUNDS ARE UNDERMINING DEBT CANCELLATION

Jubilee USA Network is extremely concerned about the impact of vulture fund activity on indebted and impoverished nations in Africa and elsewhere. Debt cancellation provides the chance for impoverished countries to start fresh and allocate additional resources to essential health, education, and other spending. Vulture funds are a real threat to the gains we have made in the debt cancellation campaign.

While the US government and the international community were extending debt relief to some impoverished countries, a new form of business emerged, with the purpose of speculating in and profiteering from poor country debt in default. This new business by so-called "vulture funds" comes at the expense of the citizens of these indebted countries—some of the poorest in the world—as well as taxpayers in countries like the US, who have been supporting in part the cost of debt relief. The Jubilee USA Network, together with partners in affected countries like Zambia, and other countries including the UK and Germany, is increasingly monitoring the activity of vulture funds and working to publicize and curtail their activity.

WHAT ARE VULTURE FUNDS? HOW DO THEY OPERATE?

'Vulture fund' is a name given to a company that seeks to make profit by buying up 'bad' debt at a cheap price, then attempts to recover the full amount, often by suing through the courts. Such companies often describe themselves as 'distressed debt funds'. Some target failing companies, but Jubilee USA Network is focused on those that target poor country governments. These vulture fund companies tend to be quite secretive, and many of them are based in tax havens. Some are owned or controlled by large, often US-based, financial institutions such as hedge funds. In other cases, there is limited or no information on who owns them. Often companies are set up simply to pursue one debt, then shut down again.

When an impoverished country has outstanding debt owed to a government or a commercial creditor—that has *not* been written down or restructured according to HIPC or MDRI terms—there is a chance that a financial organization will seek to buy that debt at reduced prices and seek repayment of the original amount and more. Firms call this capitalizing, but we as debt campaigners consider this vulture activity.

In the past several decades, vulture funds have traditionally focused their activities in middle-income countries such as Peru, where Elliott Associates pursued a lawsuit in the 1990s. But in the past 3 years, the provision of debt cancellation to HIPCs has encouraged these funds to target them as now HIPC nations have more resources—thanks to debt relief from the US government, the international financial institutions, and others. This vulture fund activity has resulted in a growing number of lawsuits being brought against HIPCs.

Before considering the scope of the problem, it is important to note that vulture creditors are not the only creditors that pose a threat to impoverished nations. Other creditors, including non-Paris Club official creditors, smaller multilateral creditors, and quasi-commercial lenders, also continue to make claims on HIPC countries. While the activities of so-called vulture funds have received the most attention, it is important to consider the full range of outstanding claims and threats that African governments are facing.

SCOPE AND IMPACT OF THE PROBLEM

According to research by Matthew Martin, Director of Debt Relief International, an NGO which works with developing country NGOs to resolve their debt crises, at least 20 Heavily Indebted Poor Countries (HIPCs) have been threatened with or have been subject to legal actions by commercial creditors and vulture funds since 1999. The debtor governments have almost always lost. There have been some mixed results and settlements out of court. The only known case where a debtor government has won in court is a case in Madagascar. When they lose, the ruling has been that the poor debtor government pay the original debt, interest and fees accrued since the debt has been in arrears, as well as the legal costs of the plaintiff.

Some of the countries that have faced legal actions by commercial creditors and vulture funds include: Angola, Bolivia, Burkina Faso, Cameroon, Republic of Congo, Cote d'Ivoire, Democratic Republic of Congo, Ethiopia, Guyana, Honduras, Madagascar, Mozambique, Nicaragua, Niger, São Tomé and Principe, Tanzania, Uganda, Yemen, and Zambia.

The amounts awarded to plaintiffs have varied from 1 to 6 times the original value of the debt, or $1 million to $153 million. The average has been 2.2 times the original value. More than 14 settlements have exceeded $50 million, a huge sum to pay in one year, especially when compared to other crucial spending needs. Considering these costs comparatively:

- In Uganda and Sierra Leone lawsuit payments were as high as 35% and 34%, respectively, of total debt service in one year.
- In Nicaragua, lawsuit cost was some $425 million in one year, only marginally less than health and education spending combined.
- In Niger, the government spent more than half of what it spent on health and education combined on lawsuits (US$76.5 million).
- In Zambia, health and education expenditure totaled almost US$303 million, while lawsuits cost almost US$127 million.

More than two-thirds of the lawsuits brought by vulture funds occur in the US or UK jurisdictions. This because is in part because these courts are seen as being more creditor-friendly and more efficient. But there are an increasing number of cases being made at the national level, where weaker legal systems get mired in the details of these cases.

Moreover, creditors often threaten impoverished countries with cases, which are then settled out of court. While there is not currently a mechanism to track these threats, one estimate is that more than $400 million has been paid out in settlements by HIPCs in the past three years alone.

THE CASE OF DONEGAL V. ZAMBIA

The most recent and visible vulture fund case has been that of Donegal International, Limited suing the government of Zambia—and winning $15 million. In 1979, Zambia purchased agricultural equipment and services from Romania on credit. Being unable to service this debt, in 1999 Zambia and Romania agreed to liquidate this debt for $3.28 million. But before Zambia could seal the deal, a vulture—Donegal International—swooped in.

Donegal International, Limited is registered in the British Virgin Islands. Its only business is to pursue the Zambian debt. Donegal's sole director is Michael Sheehan, who owns a company called Debt Advisory International, based in Washington DC. He bought this debt valued at $3.28 million and later sued the Zambian government for $55 million. On April 24th, the British High Court ruled that the government of Zambia would have to pay Donegal some $15 million. This represents over a third of what Zambia is projected to save in debt relief delivered through HIPC and the MDRI in 2007.

This case is of particular concern to Jubilee USA Network because our organization led a delegation to Zambia in early 2007, to evaluate the impacts of debt cancellation that Zambia has received under the HIPC Initiative and the MDRI. What we saw was hopeful. We visited a rural health clinic—in the Siavonga region—which had abolished user fees thanks to the debt cancellation deal. This meant that while patients in desperate need had previously been turned away, now they had access to vital care and medicines. This was a concrete and positive outcome of debt cancellation commitments.

While in Zambia, we met with the Finance Ministry and learned that Zambia would have about $40 million freed up in its national budget in 2007 thanks to the debt cancellation agreement. But with the victory by Donegal in UK courts last month, Zambia will now have to send more than a third of its debt relief savings this year—to the vultures. This is money that should be used to build more clinics, schools, and provide greater access to basic services to Zambians, not to line the pockets of a wealthy American investor.

Zambia is a clear example of the problem presented by vulture funds. But it is not the only one. We know that there are cases pending, or threats of litigation, at this very moment in Cameroon, Republic of Congo, and Liberia. Action is needed now so that what happened to Zambia will not happen to other impoverished African nations.

POLICY RESPONSES: THE BUSH ADMINISTRATION, THE G–8, AND THE US CONGRESS

The activities of vulture funds clearly undermine the debt relief agreements supported by the US government and other G–8 governments.

In 2005 at the G–8 summit in Gleneagles, Scotland, President Bush and other G–8 leaders announced a new deal on impoverished country debt which would provide "100% debt cancellation" to eligible HIPC countries—expanding beyond previous initiatives which had only provided partial debt relief to eligible nations. Jubilee USA and others welcomed this initiative as an important first step towards broader debt cancellation which is needed to fight poverty.

It is important to note that US taxpayers have been bearing the costs of this important initiative—both the costs of cancelling debts owed by these nations to our government as well as to the World Bank, through the US appropriations to the International Development Association (IDA).

But the activities of vulture funds in Zambia and elsewhere in Africa are clearly undermining US foreign economic policy and the 2005 G–8 debt deal. It is the US national interest to respond with clear proposals and action so that these cases no longer occur, and so that taxpayer funds allocated for debt relief are not used by impoverished countries to compensate vulture funds.

In recent months, in response to heightened publicity and attention from development campaigners, the Bush administration and the G–8 have begun to make statements on the threat posed by vulture funds.

Gordon Brown, the UK Chancellor and soon to be Prime Minister said in a statement in the UK Parliament on May 10, 2007, "I deplore the activities of so-called vulture funds that seek to profit from debts owed by the poorest countries in the world. I am determined to limit the damage done by such funds." Chancellor Brown also released a list of 6 specific policy proposals to address the problem.

German officials—including Chancellor Angela Merkel and Development Minister Heidi Marie Wieczroek-Zeul—have also indicated their concern about the issue in recent weeks. In a recent meeting with NGOs in Germany, Chancellor Merkel request more information on the subject for inclusion in the summit's communiqué.

The Bush administration has also expressed concern on the subject, based on the concern that these "vulture funds" are "free-riding" on the multilateral debt deal so tortuously negotiated with US leadership in 2005.

This past weekend, on May 19, 2007, G–8 Finance Ministers met in Potsdam, Germany. They responded to concerns about the activities of vulture funds by stating: "We encourage the use of the debt sustainability framework by all borrowers and creditors in their decisions. We continue to support the development of a charter for responsible lending and seek to involve other interested parties, including the G20. In this context we are concerned about the actions of some litigating creditors against Heavily Indebted Poor Countries. We have agreed to work together to identify measures to tackle this problem, based on the work of the Paris Club."

The statements of concern from the Administration and other members of the G–8 are welcome, but they must now be followed by strong action. The G–8 summit is less than three weeks from today. The G–8 should commit to specific action at the upcoming G–8 summit, which will be held in Germany from June 6–8, 2007.

Congress can play a critical role by encouraging and working with the Administration to develop and support specific policy proposals to address the challenge presented by vulture funds.

Specifically, we are calling on the Bush Administration and G–8 leaders to:

1. Urge the World Bank to more aggressively buy back outstanding commercial debts in all eligible countries to get at-risk debts out of the public domain. The World Bank should expand the IDA debt reduction facility so that it is available to Heavily Indebted Poor Countries (HIPCs) before they reach decision point and allow repeat operations for all eligible countries. Opening the

facility before decision point would be particularly helpful to Liberia, which faces more than $1 billion in hedge fund debt claims. Furthermore, the debt eligible for IDA debt reduction facility operations should also include debts owed to "semi-commercial" enterprises of non-OECD countries.

2. Support the development of codes of conduct for commercial creditors and a Charter for responsible lending which includes binding requirements that creditors not sell or re-assign sovereign debts owed by nations eligible for debt cancellation without explicit approval of the debtor.

3. Increase technical and legal assistance to all HIPCs with debts at risk. This support should be extended to prevent lawsuits from being brought against governments and to help once there is a suit.

4. Ultimately, G–8 leaders must work for changes in national laws to make vulture fund profiteering illegal.

Action is needed in the short-term while broader changes are made to truly stop the practices of vulture funds. The first three policy proposals can be accomplished quickly with support of the G–8 and international financial institutions. Meanwhile, Congress should investigate viable changes in US law which would discourage or forbid profiteering by vulture funds in the future.

A soon-to-be introduced piece of legislation, the Jubilee Act for Responsible Lending and Expanded Debt Cancellation, will likely include several provisions on the issue of vulture activity. This is one specific legislative approach that members can support while more comprehensive legislation is in development.

CONCLUSION

Debt cancellation is a critical and effective tool in the fight against poverty in Africa and across the global South. Vulture funds threaten to undermine the effectiveness of debt cancellation. Action must be taken now to ensure that the gains from debt cancellation are preserved.

While vulture funds are a critical issue, it is also important to remember that vulture funds are one piece of a broader unfinished agenda on international debt. More countries need access to the benefits of debt cancellation. According to Oxfam International, even after debt relief, low-income countries still pay $100 million each day in debt service payments in 2005. As we address the problem of vulture funds, let us also work to expand the life-saving promise of cancellation of unjust debts to all impoverished countries so that they can meet the Millennium Development Goals.

Mr. PAYNE. Well, let me thank you very much for your testimony, both of you. I would also like to point out for the record that we requested a witness from the Department of the Treasury. We requested Secretary Paulson or one of his deputies to testify at the hearing today, but he said he was unable to make it, and that they just didn't have anyone in the Treasury that was well versed on this issue. I don't know how many people work for the Treasury Department, but he said that there was no one well versed because there is a United States-China strategic economic dialogue that is started this week, so I guess everyone is over studying China. But to have a department, our U.S. Treasury Department to say that there is no one who is well versed on the issue who can attend this hearing leaves a lot to be desired.

Let me say that I, as I indicated earlier, when I did, after hearing the BBC, to hear Amy Goodman on Democracy Now that morning on my way to the two meetings I mentioned, and did mention with President Bush, he did seem to have some interest on some of the points that we raised, and so hopefully we can maybe perhaps get the administration to look at it. He really expressed some real concern about it. Maybe we will just need the Treasury Department alone.

Let me ask you just in regard to the Zambia case, do you feel that the attorneys for the Government of Zambia were sort of at a disadvantage? What can you tell us about the case or what do you think might have been an unfair sort of situation that they found themselves in?

Ms. WOODS. Well, first, when you think about the developing world, but particularly the African governments, a large percentage of the issues are around capacity, and often the capacity of government to be able to provide technical assistance on a range of issues from trade negotiations to environmental protection, there is a range of issues on the plate.

In the case of Zambia, the first question was, can there be adequate legal advice and technical assistance brought to bear on this case to be able to actually prevent it from going to court, advancing, and then to be able to actually win the case?

So in response to your question, I think the first constraint is the financial resources. The legal fees are incredibly high, and countries that are already strapped with the debt and debt service payments that they are making are finding it more and more difficult to pour resources that really should be going toward schools and hospitals, and toward the improvement of the standard of living in their country, and to instead pour those resources into lawyers' fees, how do you even justify it politically?

So the financial constraint, and then the technical constraints posed by these cases are tremendous, and they should not be overlooked.

In addition to that, you have a case being presented in another country, and the jurisdiction of another country, the travel cost to that other country, all of these associated fees make it increasingly difficult for adequate representation to occur.

But the bigger picture really is the power of the financial markets and the power of the corporations, and often times it is the African governments that are facing the financial markets, and in particular in this cases, very wealthy investors who end up having the upper hand in these legal cases. So there is an issue of the dominance of corporate power and what that brings into a circumstance of inequity like these cases.

Mr. PAYNE. Thank you very much.

Mr. Watkins, according to your testimony, you stated that over $400 million have been paid to vulture funds in the past 3 years. How much money is at stake here, and how much debt could possibly get in the hands of these vulture funds if they were able to win them all?

Mr. WATKINS. There is a significant amount at stake. Just in the past 3 years, you refer to the figure of $400 million. If you look at since 1999, we understand that there have been $2 billion in claims against HIPCs from commercial creditors and vulture creditors. So this is a serious, this is a serious amount of money.

I think that as things move forward we should be aware that the G–8 debt deal, which was negotiated in 2005, has provided between $40 billion and $50 billion of debt cancellation to impoverished countries, so there is a significant amount of debt which has been canceled. What is left is debt that is commercial debt, it is debt which is owed to non-Paris Club official creditors, so that is governments that aren't part of the Paris Club. It is owed to these quasi-commercial lenders, so that vulture funds are really part of a bigger picture.

As we negotiate debt cancellation in the future, we need to make sure that it is a comprehensive approach; that as the U.S. Governments makes a commitment, or the IMF and World Bank make a commitment to debt cancellation, that other creditors should be encouraged, should be more than just encouraged, they should really be pushed to be included in those initiatives or else you are going to have more and more problems like this.

Mr. PAYNE. Okay, just my final question, and we will hear from Congressman Tancredo.

Some private financial institutions have complained that they do not have significant enough role in formal credit or groups like the Paris Club. What role do private financial institutions play in debt restructuring? Does their possible exclusion, in your opinion, play a role in how vulture funds are able to operate today?

Ms. WOODS. I think the biggest issue for the developing countries and dealing with their debt is the amount owed to the international financial institutions, the World Bank, the International Monetary Fund, the regional banks, and dealing with those debts would lift a tremendous burden from the developing countries, and free up much needed resources for the building block of development.

I think opening up to further activity from commercial investors is not necessarily a good thing. Again, our bigger picture here is getting the economies back on track, and what is needed actually is creation of jobs, it is opening up schools, building hospitals, to build for the long-term sustainable future of countries so that the assets within the country can be unleashed for the development of that country, and to meet the needs of the country so that you don't have to go either to the international financial institutions or to private creditors to actually balance accounts and bring financial stability.

So ultimately what we want, we recognize particularly in Africa the richness of the continent, we recognize the massive resources—Zambia's copper, Liberian's rubber, gold, diamond, and timber. I mean, the resources are tremendous, and what is needed is actually to use those resources in the benefit of the country, to benefit the citizens of the country.

So we need to think about opportunities that bring perhaps taxation of activity, corporate activity and others that will bring government revenue in a sustainable way so that governments don't have to rely on foreign creditors to actually balance their books.

Mr. PAYNE. Thank you very much.

Mr. Tancredo.

Mr. TANCREDO. Thank you, Mr. Chairman.

Actually, it is not just the Department of Treasury that doesn't know a lot about this, I must admit to you until you called this hearing I was really not familiar with even the term "vulture funds," and so it is really quite enlightening, very interesting, and I appreciate the fact that you have called the hearing.

By the way, let me ask your forgiveness for these here. I am not listening to a game or anything. I have an ear problem and this is a device that is supposed to help, so I don't want you to think I am not paying attention to you, and I can hear everything that you said.

The issue of transparency and accountability, though, is an important one for developing nations in acquiring foreign loans, and it may—if we had more of it, it may do something to stop the ability of these vulture funds, as I understand it, and for instance, Zambia would be a case.

Wouldn't that be something we would have to look at or could look at as a way of dealing with this, and by the way would not be just something that would make it more difficult for vulture funds? It would make it better for the flow of private capital into the countries themselves if we would do more to encourage transparency and accountability in any of these developing countries. Isn't that one part of it?

Then just another thing I was thinking of while we were talking about it, there is a huge flow of private capital into developing countries through a variety of different mechanisms. These vulture funds account for—I don't know what percentage of all, but I worry that what we may do in order to stop what appears to be kind of an unacceptable practice would also inhibit the flow in some way of let us say good foreign investment and capital investment that we would otherwise want to encourage.

It is very difficult sometimes to actually cut that slice so clearly that you make sure that you are taking the one out without doing something unintended, the law of unintended consequences, I guess.

Those two things, and either of you can answer it for me.

Mr. WATKINS. Thank you for both questions. I think they are very critical issues.

First on transparency and accountability, I think we as Jubilee see two sides to that coin: That there should be transparency and accountability from the lenders and from the creditors, but also from the borrowers. So how do you make sure there is a good mix?

One of the concerns we have had about the build-up of the debt crisis is that a lot of these loans were made many years ago, decades ago, and they were made—unaccountably they were made to dictators, they were made to regimes which were unsavory but perhaps were of strategic interest to various countries that were making the loans. So we think that there needs to be an audit, that the books of the IMF, the World Bank, some of these lending agencies should be opened up and that we look at what some of the actual criteria were for these loans and whether these were indeed transparent and accountable loans that were made.

The parallel to that is that the borrower side. Obviously, there needs to be transparency and accountability by countries which are borrowing, which are receiving funds from the IMF and World Bank. We have seen from the debt relief that has come to date, that that is a feature. That in order to receive debt cancellation countries do need to show that the funds are being used for productive purposes, for health care, for education, and we have seen the impact on the ground of some of those programs.

So I think that is a very important pieces as we campaign for broader cancellation, one of the key pieces we are looking at is how to make sure countries actually use the funds they receive for debt cancellation to fight poverty, and that is a combination of both requirements but also civil society in those countries holding their own governments accountable.

I visited Zambia in January.

Mr. TANCREDO. Yes.

Mr. WATKINS. And I was very impressed by what is called Civil Society for Poverty Reduction. It is a coalition of dozens of organizations that are holding their government's feet to the fire, watching the budget, watching the Parliament, making sure they are doing what they are supposed to be doing. It is not perfect, but it is what we would do in this country. We hold our own government accountable, and that is, I think, some of the strongest force.

On the second question, on the flow of private capital, obviously we want to make sure that we are not stopping so-called good capital and investment. We want to make sure that we are really going after those that are ruthless, and I think there is a difference between legitimate investment, foreign direct investment, and vulture creditors, which are clearly on the market in order to purchase debts and then sue the country, and then try to get even more money than they purchased the debt for because that is a special class.

So I think in some of the remedies that I proposed it was looking at how to address that particular class, though I think we also do need in some sense to allow countries to regulate the flows of investments into their country to make sure they are beneficial to the people.

Ms. WOODS. Well, if I may add. Congressman Tancredo, thank you for being here and for acknowledging lack of familiarity with this issue. I think we are thrilled that you take the time to engage in this issue, and I hope you hear from us a sense of urgency to get others to engage as well.

On the question of investment, clearly Africa is being looked to for foreign direct investment. It is not just the United States, it is China, Malaysia, India, the list is growing, because of the vital and strategic resources of the continent. What we are proposing is not to constrain the investment, but actually I believe your two questions are linked because essentially where they come together is that in order for investment to be unleashed in positive ways that bring development, that bring growth, you need the transparency, you need accountability on both ends, both on the ends of the African governments and counterparts, and on the end of the corporate actors.

So more transparency is what we want when we think about oil extraction, for example, in Nigeria, the claims are really for greater transparency. It is not only oil, but all of the industries with the understanding that under the light of day you do not have deals being made behind closed doors and under the table that may benefit elites either in the African country or elites here or internationally, and yet not benefit the people.

So what we are calling for, particularly in an era of new leadership coming forward on the continent, is a commitment to real transparency, to real accountability that will look to both ends, at corporate activity and at the investors overall, as well as look at government responsibility in that end.

Mr. TANCREDO. Thank you, Mr. Chairman.

Ms. Woods. Thank you.

Mr. Payne. Thank you.

Ms. Watson?

Ms. Watson. These for-profit firms, and thank you so much for being a panelist, and Mr. Watkins, we appreciate it, these firms that are offering the vulture funding, do you know what their overhead costs might be?

Now, they are for a profit, and so how much of that goes into the overhead, added to the interest on these funds that creates the debt? Do you have any idea?

Ms. Woods. Well, if you think about these funds, it is really like a shell game. It is hard to know who is with which fund, where they are based. You have people registering in British Virgin Islands, United States registered.

Ms. Watson. Is it like an arbitrage?

Ms. Woods. It is really a shell game. You may have one person responsible for several different funds under several different names, registered in countries all over the world. So it is hard to actually pin down how much would be their actual cost, their real costs, and how much inflated.

But essentially what is happening is the debt is being bought at a very low rate, and then the countries are being sued for the face value of that debt.

Ms. Watson. Yes.

Ms. Woods. So it is egregious if you think about it. It should be a foreign corrupt practice to be able to kind of charge such usury rates.

Now, here in the domestic context we talk about these sub prime loans and the impact that they are having on poor communities.

Ms. Watson. Yes.

Ms. Woods. Well, it is a similar phenomenon happening in the international scene where poor countries are being opened up to these vultures, essentially taking them for all they have got.

So I don't know the amount of their overhead. I suspect that they too are pouring tremendous amounts into these legal fees, you know, as these cases mount, but clearly when you win a case as Donegal did in the U.K. you get back far more than you invested, and the vultures could continue along this path if they are not stopped.

Ms. Watson. I am really pleased that the chair has brought this issue to our attention, and I would think, in terms of recommendations, Mr. Chair, that we ought to take this to a higher level because what it is doing is forcing these poor developing countries further into debt, and more challenges that they could be using to reconstruct and to build up.

So I think we ought to find a way, and where would be the proper place? I mean, the G–8, maybe, you know, wherever so that we can focus—like how do we help these developing countries in Africa, and I see a future for that continent within the next few years because that is where we are going to be looking for the resources that we used to depend on the Middle East. We are going to go to Africa, so that they would be able to benefit from the new business and attention that we ought to bring this to a higher level, maybe to the U.N., and to discuss it, and if we want to truly see these countries develop and they are using funds that we know are going to burden them down, somebody comes along and buys them in the secondary market, it just makes it more and more difficult for them.

So I think you have shed some light on a subject that I think needs to go beyond our committee here, and I guess that is the reason why we are having this hearing, and I thank the chair for bringing it to our attention, but I would like to see us do more with this in the national arena.

Mr. PAYNE. Right, thank you.

Yes, earlier we mentioned that I have been in conversation with Congressman Conyers, chairman of the Judiciary Committee, which has responsibility, and also Chairman Barney Frank for financial services, and so Mr. Conyers is already scheduling a hearing. Mr. Frank's committee is investigating it. We will send a letter to the President from our committee urging him to raise this issue at the G–8 summit coming up in June. So whether he will or not, that is another question, but we will certainly ask that to happen.

The gentlelady from Texas, Ms. Jackson Lee.

Ms. JACKSON LEE. I want to thank the witnesses for their appearance today, and I add my appreciation to the chairman of the committee, and ranking member for bringing it.

Danny Glover mentioned in his testimony that vulture funds destroy the benefits of debt relief. I would like to add to that, and he might as well, that debt relief destroys the country itself. The vulture destroys the country itself as well, these vulture funds. And I particularly think of Ms. Johnson, as you mentioned, in Liberia with the short window that she has to turn around the country, not because of her outstanding talents, but because of the expectations of the people.

So I would like to build upon the thought that have been represented by my colleagues, and just simply ask the question. What do you think the United Nations could do, one? And two, many of these vulture companies only listen to a direct, if you will, affront, or questioning of their ability to do business, and so out of the hearings would you think that legislation that points itself to the vulture funds and their ability to do business in the United States or whether they are European based, their building to do business in Europe would be the approach to take because I, frankly, don't believe any sort of cooperative spirit would in any way move them to do the right thing?

For example, as you said, when the United States gives that relief to have a larger net to bring them in, I think they will only respond to what keeps them from doing business period. So I welcome your thoughts and whether we need punitive measures to wake up these vulture funds to realize that what they do destroys a country as opposed to helps a country. Ms. Woods?

Ms. WOODS. Well, thank you for your comments and the sentiments of them, and also for your question. I think when it comes to the punitive issues, clearly there is need for legislation here. When we see especially the escalating amounts that these vulture funds are generating in terms of income being really diverted from the developing world, I think this is an activity that needs regulation. It cries out for regulation.

So we would very much support a legislative solution that looks to actually curbing these practices that we believe are foreign corrupt practices, and to actually putting forward punitive measures where you cannot continue this type of egregious activity around the world, with concrete measures to stop such illicit and immoral practices.

In addition, I think we are also very supportive of actually buying out the debt and making sure that there are measures put in place through instructions to Treasury, which can come from this committee, that actually take away the opportunities for these types of practices to happen in the future. So there is a way that you deal with the current problem and you take away future opportunities to engage in these types of activities.

But the third step is actually encouraging an internationally binding agreement where you bring together the debtors and the creditors in one place, almost like a Chapter 11-type hearing where you have a fair and transparent process where the debts are put on the table, and there is an open process where the public in the developing country can also participate in the process, a process that has both a U.S. national as well as an international component to it too.

So we think these measures would go a long way toward preventing these types of activities in the future.

Ms. JACKSON LEE. Mr. Watkins, do you have a quick answer?

Mr. WATKINS. Sure.

Ms. JACKSON LEE. Sorry about the bells going off.

Mr. WATKINS. Sure. Just very briefly I think you need a multipronged approach. I think we can make demands of the G–8. This is an initiative, the debt relief initiative, which they created a couple of years ago so they should, I feel, feel compunction to take specific measures in the next few weeks as they meet.

Second, that ultimately legislative approaches will also be critical, and I think there are two things. One, there is the Jubilee Act for Responsible Lending and Expanded Debt Cancellation, which will be introduced soon, which will have some measures on vultures, specifically calling on Treasury to take action.

Then we also believe that a stronger piece of legislation focused on vultures themselves and the legal aspect of what in U.S. law allows them to operate this way should also move forward.

So there are, I think, a multiple-pronged approach would be most effective.

Ms. JACKSON LEE. Thank you. Thank you, Mr. Chairman. Yield back.

Mr. PAYNE. Thank you very much, and we might look at the camera on the Cameroon/Chad pipeline, the way that they were able to look to the World Bank, put in conditionality actually on how the funds from the oil could be spent in Chad for infrastructures, education, et cetera. So I think there are some examples that we could look at.

Let me thank you all again, and we will continue to work with you. The meeting stands adjourned.

[Whereupon, at 4:05 p.m., the subcommittee was adjourned.]

APPENDIX

MATERIAL SUBMITTED FOR THE HEARING RECORD

PREPARED STATEMENT OF THE HONORABLE SHEILA JACKSON LEE, A REPRESENTATIVE IN CONGRESS FROM THE STATE OF TEXAS

Thank you, Mr. Chairman, for convening today's extremely important hearing. Nearly two years ago, we saw an outpouring of support for debt relief as G8 leaders met in Gleneagles, Scotland, to pursue a policy of poverty reduction. While some positive progress has been made since that meeting, it is absolutely undeniable that this is an issue on which a great deal remains to be done. May I also thank the Ranking Member of the subcommittee, and welcome our four distinguished witnesses: Danny Glover, the Chairman of the Board of the TransAfrica Forum, Inc.; Emira Woods, Co-Director of Foreign Policy in Focus at the Institute for Policy Studies; and Neil Watkins, National Coordinator of Jubilee USA Network. I look forward to your testimony.

Mr. Chairman, the term "vulture funds" invokes images of a spectral bird, circling its dying prey. It is not in our interest to leave any members of the international community as carcasses to be picked clean by opportunistic investors. Instead, the international community has developed several initiatives aimed at reducing debt in the world's poorest countries, and thus freeing up resources to help these nations reach the United Nations' Millennium Development Goals (MDGs). As a member of Congress, I have actively supported debt relief, and it remains my firm belief that without some degree of debt cancellation it will be very difficult to bring many developing nations into the global market.

Though most developed nations have pursued some form of debt relief, vulture funds have, like their avian namesakes, sought to make a profit off of already weakened prey. These investment funds purchase the debt of countries (or companies) in financial distress. They then hold out for the full value of the debt, plus any interest, which they pursue through litigation, much of which takes place in U.S. courts. Vulture funds also operate in the secondary debt market.

Countries throughout Africa suffer from the heavy burden of debt. The inability of nations to escape from these financial commitments has profound impacts on any attempts they make at poverty reduction, health care, economic development, and sustainable growth. The Highly Indebted Poor Countries (HIPCs), the majority of which are located in Africa, are particularly crippled by debt. Though these countries may not appear to be the most profitable prey for vulture funds, which in theory prefer to purchase debt that a country has, or may in the future develop, the ability to pay, according to reports there are numerous lawsuits currently pending against HIPC countries.

International investment funds are often attracted to developing countries, where plentiful investment opportunities coupled with a scarcity of domestic investment funds drives interest rates up. Increased investment, and the resultant flow of capital into the country, can bring important economic benefits for developing countries, including a rising GPD and higher productivity and living standards. However, creditors may pull out when they lose confidence in the country's ability to repay, worsening the economic decline that caused the initial doubts.

Vulture funds undermine international efforts to provide much needed debt relief to the world's most indebted poor countries. The United States alone has forgiven $23.9 billion in foreign debt since 1991; likewise, the international community, including the IMF and the World Bank, as well as a group of major creditor nations known collectively as the Paris Club, has taken major steps to provide much needed debt relief as part of broader poverty reduction programs. The HIPC Initiative of the World Bank and the IMF, in particular, stipulates that any funds freed up by debt relief must be used explicitly for poverty reduction efforts.

(29)

Despite recent landmark cases involving vulture funds, the application of legal principles on this issue has not been firmly established. The concept of "odious debt" has become a contentious issue, with many legal scholars suggesting that "those predecessor obligations 'which are contracted contrary to the interests of the inhabitants of the absorbed territory'" are not binding on successor governments. This is contrary to classical theories of international law, but not to classical practice of our own nation, which, when conquering territory including my own state of Texas, refused to take on liability for that territory's debts. More recent efforts by the United Nations to codify international law on this subject never gained sufficient ratifications to enter into effect. However, two recent cases, *Elliot Associates, L.P.* v. *Banco de la Nacion & Republic of Peru*, and *Donegal International Ltd.* v. *Republic of Zambia* have both ruled in favor of the investment fund.

Mr. Chairman, vulture funds are harmful to our efforts to promote sustainable international development, and to reduce poverty around the world. I would urge this committee to actively engage with this topic, and to consider options to limit this predatory behavior. Additionally, since debt relief will not solve the underlying economic and political conditions that worsen the ability of many African nations to pursue long-term development strategies, I urge this committee, and this Congress, to consider debt relief and development within this larger paradigm.

I very much look forward to the testimony of our panel of witnesses, and to further discussions of this issue with my colleagues. Thank you, Mr. Chairman, and I yield back the balance of my time.

○

CPSIA information can be obtained at www.ICGtesting.com
Printed in the USA
BVOW01s1943051016

464257BV00008B/91/P